emotional rescue

STUDIO PRESS BOOKS

First published in the UK in 2018 by Studio Press Books,
an imprint of Kings Road Publishing, part of Bonnier Books UK,
The Plaza, 535 King's Road, London, SW10 0SZ

www.studiopressbooks.co.uk
www.bonnierbooks.co.uk

Printed Under License ©2018 Emotional Rescue
www.emotional-rescue.com

3 5 7 9 10 8 6 4

ISBN 978-1-78741-339-9

Printed in Turkey

The Wit & Wisdom of
GIN

**STUDIO
PRESS**

"Hand me the Gin!" said Emma. "Because no good story starts with 'that one time I ate salad.'"

Samantha has one glass of Gin for health benefits.
(The rest are for witty remarks and amazing dance moves!)

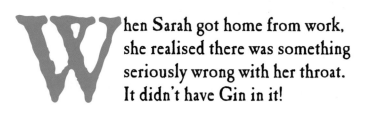

When Sarah got home from work, she realised there was something seriously wrong with her throat. It didn't have Gin in it!

For Gail, the most expensive part of having kids, is all the Gin you have to drink!

As far as Elaine was concerned, Birthdays were nature's way of telling you to drink more Gin!!

It was Fiona's zest for life and generous disposition that had kept her young and happy over the years. Well, that and Gin!

Tabitha mixed herself a Birthday cocktail!
10% milk for her complexion,
15% vitamins for health and
75% Gin so she wouldn't give a toss!

"A good man can make you feel sexy, strong and able to take on the world!" said Susan, "Oh no, sorry! That's Gin... Gin does that!"

"**I** really do love you, you're my best friend in the whole world!"

"Is that the Gin talking?" asked her friend.

"No, it's me talking to the Gin!"

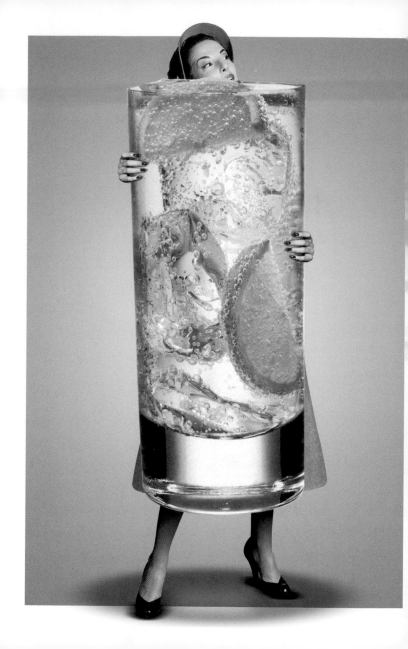

Claire was finding it really hard to hold her Gin!

After several G&Ts on her Birthday, Sally bid everyone a slurred goodnight and made a dramatic exit into a cupboard.

Never again would the little sod hide her Mum's Gin!

Tina liked big Gins and she could not lie.

At the top of her Birthday wish-list, Michelle put a bottle of teqiu... teuqul... Gin!!

At last, Gina had finally discovered something that truly took the drudgery out of washdays.

Having to work on her Birthday was made a lot more bearable when her friend thought of a foolproof way to smuggle Gin into the office.

Mum wasn't the sort of woman to cry over spilt milk.
But spilt Gin however, was a *totally* different matter!

If ever she felt sad about being another year older, she would just Gin and bear it!

It looked like someone had put too much tonic in Cecelia's Gin again.

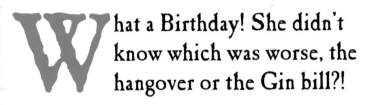

What a Birthday! She didn't know which was worse, the hangover or the Gin bill?!

Mary had just read so much about the terrible effects of both chocolate and Gin that she immediately decided to give up reading.

Penelope's use of Gin was 'medicinal'... she drank it because she was sick of her kids!

Sarah was a girl of very few words. Mainly: Gin, Yes and Please!

They shared everything together — thoughts, feelings, secrets and more often than not, three bottles of Gin.